This book belongs to

_____

- -

_____

_____

- -

_____

TABLE OF CONTENTS

Part 1:
What is cursive handwriting?

Cursive handwriting can be any writing style where letters are connected to create a flowing manner.

Interestingly, it can reveal a lot about a person's personality, mood, and even physical state. Handwriting analysts examine various features of a person's handwriting, such as the size, shape, slant, and pressure of the letters, to gain insights into their character and behavior. For example, large handwriting can indicate an outgoing and confident personality, while small handwriting may depict introversion and attention to detail. A right slant can suggest optimism and sociability, while a left slant is believed to reveal introspection and reserve. Heavy pressure on the pen or pencil can display strong emotions, while light pressure tends to show a gentle and sensitive nature.

It's important to note that these generalizations are not a scientifically proven method of personality assessment. However, handwriting can still be beneficial to us, especially during our teenage years for the following reasons:

- Cursive handwriting helps save time. The letters flow together, reducing the time needed to lift the pen or pencil and start a new letter. In today's fast-paced world, being able to write quickly and efficiently is a valuable skill.

- Cursive handwriting can improve hand-eye coordination and fine motor skills. Writing in cursive requires precise and controlled movements of the hand and fingers, which can enhance dexterity and coordination.

- Cursive handwriting creates your aesthetic and personal values. Many people find cursive writing elegant and attractive, and it can be a way for them to express their personality and creativity.

A lot of schools don't teach cursive anymore and this style of writing doesn't seem to have the importance it once did. But if you have always wanted to learn, this workbook is designed especially for you.

You can see cursive handwriting everywhere, and whenever it appears, it can make a difference in the world of screens and keyboards.

Find joy in simple things!

Jack

Fairuz

Sign

Dear diary...

Life can be so confusing sometimes. It feels like every day there are new challenges to face and decisions to make. Some days, I feel like I have everything figured out, and other days I feel lost and uncertain.

Today was one of those uncertain days. I found out that I didn't make the cut for the school play that I was really looking forward to. It's not the end of the world, but it's still disappointing. I put so much effort into my audition, and I thought I did pretty well. I guess I just wasn't good enough.

It's hard not to compare myself to others sometimes. I see my classmates getting lead roles or getting accepted into prestigious programs, and I wonder if I'm just not as talented or smart as they are. But I know that's not true. Everyone has their own strengths and weaknesses, and just because I didn't get this particular opportunity doesn't mean that I won't find other opportunities in the future.

The menu

APPETIZERS
Tuna Tartare
Petite Crab Cakes

ENTREES
Pan Roasted Salmon
Bone-in Prime Ribeye
Herb Roasted Turkey Breast

DESSERTS
Chocolate Mousse
Berries and Cream

DRINKS
Red Wine
Sparkling Water

John + Linda

INVITE YOU TO THEIR WEDDING!

12TH SEPTEMBER 2023 / 3PM
GRAND HOTEL
23 MAIN STREET

Dinner and dancing to follow

Part 2:
Before you start

If you want to improve your cursive handwriting, it's important to set aside time each day for practice. One effective method is to commit to writing at least one page per day. This can be done with a simple pen and paper or through specialized handwriting practice books.

When practicing, it's important to focus on proper letter formation, spacing, and connections between letters. Start by writing each letter of the alphabet in cursive, ensuring that each letter is formed correctly. Once you are comfortable with individual letters, move on to writing words and eventually full sentences.

It can also be helpful to find examples of cursive handwriting that you admire and use them as a guide for your own practice. Pay attention to the shape and flow of the letters and try to replicate them in your own handwriting.

Consistency is key when it comes to improving your cursive handwriting. Make a habit of practicing each day, even if it's just for a few minutes. Over time, you'll notice your handwriting becoming more legible, fluid, and attractive. With patience and dedication, anyone can develop strong cursive handwriting skills.

Consistency is key in cursive handwriting practice.

Which pen to choose?

Generally, gel pens and fine-liner pens are both good options. Don't pick a pencil or a ballpoint pen because they aren't smooth and you will need to press very hard.

How to sit to write comfortably?

When practicing handwriting, it's important to sit in a comfortable and supportive position that allows you to focus on your writing without straining your body.
Here are some tips for you when practicing cursive handwriting:

- Sit at a table or desk that is at a comfortable height for you. Make sure your feet are flat on the ground and your knees are at a 90-degree angle.
- Use a chair that provides good back support. You want to be sitting up straight but not so rigid that it causes tension in your shoulders or neck.
- Keep your writing surface at a slight angle, around 20-30 degrees. This will allow better control and prevent your hand from cramping.
- Position your paper so that it's centered in front of you, and don't have to twist your body or neck to write.
- Use proper lighting to reduce strain on your eyes. Natural light is best. In case that's not possible, use a lamp. If you are right-handed, the lamp should be on your left and vice versa so that it's going to shine on your paper without creating shadows.
- Remember to take breaks and stretch your hands and arms if you start to feel any discomfort.

With regular practice and a comfortable sitting position, you'll be on your way to improving your cursive handwriting skills in no time.

Part 3: Letters

a a a a a a a a

a a a a a a a a

a

a

A A A A A A A

A A A A A A A

A

A

b

B

𝒞 ↗   c   c   c   c   c   c   c   c   c

c   c   c   c   c   c   c   c   c

c

c

𝒞 →   e   e   e   e   e   e

e   e   e   e   e   e

e

e

a b c **d** e f g h i j k l m n o p q r s t u v w x y z

d 1 2

d d d d d d d d
d d d d d d d d

d

d

D

D D D D D D D
D D D D D D D

D

D

A B C **D** E F G H I J K L M N O P Q R S T U V W X Y Z

e

e e e e e e e e

e e e e e e e e

e

e

E

E E E E E E E E

E E E E E E E E

E

E

g

G G G G G G G G
G G G G G G G G
G
G

G G G G G G G
G G G G G G G
G
G

h

h h h h h h h h h h h
h h h h h h h h h h h
h
h

H

H H H H H H H H
H H H H H H H H
H
H

i

i

i

J

J

J

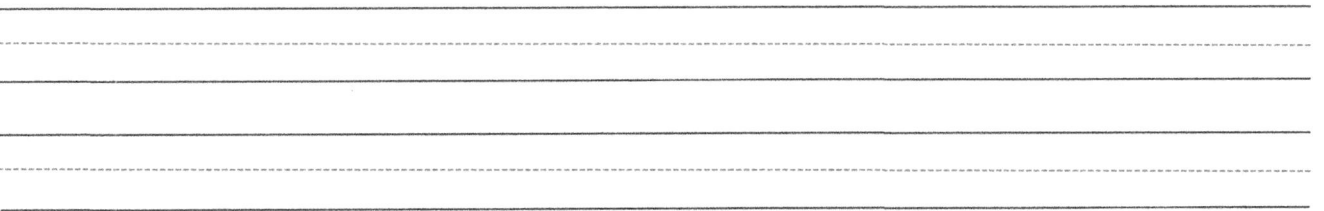

k

k k k k k k k k k

k k k k k k k k k

k

k

K

K K K K K K K

K K K K K K K

K

K

ℓ ℓ ℓ ℓ ℓ ℓ ℓ ℓ ℓ ℓ ℓ

ℓ ℓ ℓ ℓ ℓ ℓ ℓ ℓ ℓ ℓ

ℓ

ℓ

𝓛 𝓛 𝓛 𝓛 𝓛 𝓛 𝓛 𝓛

𝓛 𝓛 𝓛 𝓛 𝓛 𝓛 𝓛

𝓛

𝓛

m

m m m m m m m m

m m m m m m m m

m

m

M

M M M M M M M

M M M M M M M

M

M

n

N

O

O O O O O O O O O

O O O O O O O O O

O

O

O

O O O O O O O

O O O O O O O

O

O

p

p p p p p p p p p

p p p p p p p p p

p

p

P

P P P P P P P

P P P P P P P

P

P

q *q* *q* *q* *q* *q* *q* *q* *q* *q*

q *q* *q* *q* *q* *q* *q* *q* *q* *q*

q

q

Q *Q* *Q* *Q* *Q* *Q* *Q*

Q *Q* *Q* *Q* *Q* *Q* *Q*

Q

Q

r

𝓇

𝓇

𝓇

ℛ

ℛ

ℛ

t   l   l   l   l   l   l   l   l   l

l   l   l   l   l   l   l   l   l   l

t

t

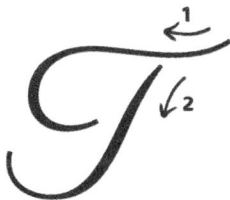

T T T T T T T T T

T T T T T T T T T

T

T

𝒰 u u u u u u u u

u u u u u u u u

u

u

𝒰 U U U U U U U

U U U U U U U

U

U

v

v

v

V

V

V

w

w

w

W

W

W

x x x x x x x x x

x x x x x x x x x

x

x

𝓧 𝓧 𝓧 𝓧 𝓧 𝓧

𝓧 𝓧 𝓧 𝓧 𝓧 𝓧

𝓧

𝓧

y y y y y y y y y y y
y y y y y y y y y y y
y
y

Y Y Y Y Y Y Y
Y Y Y Y Y Y Y
Y
Y

Part 4: Words

apple apple apple apple apple

action action action action action

alive alive alive alive alive

book book book book book

bestie bestie bestie bestie bestie

brave brave brave brave brave

clock clock clock clock clock

choice choice choice choice choice

candy candy candy candy candy

duck duck duck duck duck

daily daily daily daily daily

deer deer deer deer deer

eager eager eager eager eager

empty empty empty empty empty

enjoy enjoy enjoy enjoy enjoy

farmer farmer farmer farmer farmer

apple

action

alive

book

bestie

brave

clock

choice

candy

duck

daily

deer

eager

empty

enjoy

farmer

faith   faith   faith   faith   faith

fresh   fresh   fresh   fresh   fresh

goal   goal   goal   goal   goal

great   great   great   great   great

ginger   ginger   ginger   ginger   ginger

happy   happy   happy   happy   happy

home   home   home   home   home

hope   hope   hope   hope   hope

ink   ink   ink   ink   ink

image   image   image   image   image

idea   idea   idea   idea   idea

juice   juice   juice   juice   juice

jolly   jolly   jolly   jolly   jolly

jump   jump   jump   jump   jump

keen   keen   keen   keen   keen

kindle   kindle   kindle   kindle   kindle

faith

fresh

goal

great

ginger

happy

home

hope

ink

image

idea

juice

jolly

jump

keen

kindle

king king king king king

learn learn learn learn learn

laugh laugh laugh laugh laugh

loyal loyal loyal loyal loyal

movie movie movie movie movie

motion motion motion motion motion

magic magic magic magic magic

nature nature nature nature nature

night night night night night

novel novel novel novel novel

ocean ocean ocean ocean ocean

outdoor outdoor outdoor outdoor outdoor

origin origin origin origin origin

paper paper paper paper paper

play play play play play

pearl pearl pearl pearl pearl

king

learn

laugh

loyal

movie

motion

magic

nature

night

novel

ocean

outdoor

origin

paper

play

pearl

quick   quick   quick   quick   quick

quiet   quiet   quiet   quiet   quiet

quest   quest   quest   quest   quest

rainy   rainy   rainy   rainy   rainy

radiant   radiant   radiant   radiant   radiant

risky   risky   risky   risky   risky

smile   smile   smile   smile   smile

strong   strong   strong   strong   strong

sporty   sporty   sporty   sporty   sporty

think   think   think   think   think

theme   theme   theme   theme   theme

trust   trust   trust   trust   trust

unique   unique   unique   unique   unique

unity   unity   unity   unity   unity

unicorn   unicorn   unicorn   unicorn   unicorn

vision   vision   vision   vision   vision

quick

quiet

quest

rainy

radiant

risky

smile

strong

sporty

think

theme

trust

unique

unity

unicorn

vision

veggie veggie veggie veggie veggie

victory victory victory victory victory

wisdom wisdom wisdom wisdom wisdom

witty witty witty witty witty

whale whale whale whale whale

x-ray x-ray x-ray x-ray x-ray

xerox xerox xerox xerox xerox

xylophone xylophone xylophone

yellow yellow yellow yellow yellow

yearn yearn yearn yearn yearn

youth youth youth youth youth

zoo zoo zoo zoo zoo

zesty zesty zesty zesty zesty

zoom zoom zoom zoom zoom

veggie

victory

wisdom

witty

whale

x-ray

xerox

xylophone

yellow

yearn

youth

zoo

zesty

zoom

Asian Asian Asian Asian Asian

Art Art Art Art Art

Able Able Able Able Able

Bird Bird Bird Bird Bird

Blue Blue Blue Blue Blue

Baby Baby Baby Baby Baby

Cake Cake Cake Cake Cake

Cute Cute Cute Cute Cute

City City City City City

Dark Dark Dark Dark Dark

Drink Drink Drink Drink Drink

Drum Drum Drum Drum Drum

East East East East East

Exam Exam Exam Exam Exam

Editor Editor Editor Editor Editor

Finn Finn Finn Finn Finn

Asian

Art

Able

Bird

Blue

Baby

Cake

Cute

City

Dark

Drink

Drum

East

Exam

Editor

Finn

Fast Fast Fast Fast Fast

Frame Frame Frame Frame Frame

Game Game Game Game Game

Gold Gold Gold Gold Gold

Good Good Good Good Good

Home Home Home Home Home

Hat Hat Hat Hat Hat

Hero Hero Hero Hero Hero

Icon Icon Icon Icon Icon

Iron Iron Iron Iron Iron

Italy Italy Italy Italy Italy

Japan Japan Japan Japan Japan

Join Join Join Join Join

Joke Joke Joke Joke Joke

Kent Kent Kent Kent Kent

Kiss Kiss Kiss Kiss Kiss

Fast

Frame

Game

Gold

Good

Home

Hat

Hero

Icon

Iron

Italy

Japan

Join

Joke

Kent

Kiss

Kate Kate Kate Kate Kate

Lion Lion Lion Lion Lion

Louis Louis Louis Louis Louis

Lily Lily Lily Lily Lily

Max Max Max Max Max

Mia Mia Mia Mia Mia

Matt Matt Matt Matt Matt

Nick Nick Nick Nick Nick

Note Note Note Note Note

Nora Nora Nora Nora Nora

Oath Oath Oath Oath Oath

Ohio Ohio Ohio Ohio Ohio

Olivia Olivia Olivia Olivia Olivia

Page Page Page Page Page

Peter Peter Peter Peter Peter

Phil Phil Phil Phil Phil

Kate

Lion

Louis

Lily

Max

Mia

Matt

Nick

Note

Nora

Oath

Ohio

Olivia

Page

Peter

Phil

Quin Quin Quin Quin Quin

Quiz Quiz Quiz Quiz Quiz

Queen Queen Queen Queen Queen

Rise Rise Rise Rise Rise

Ryan Ryan Ryan Ryan Ryan

Ruby Ruby Ruby Ruby Ruby

Sam Sam Sam Sam Sam

Sean Sean Sean Sean Sean

Seoul Seoul Seoul Seoul Seoul

Tune Tune Tune Tune Tune

Talk Talk Talk Talk Talk

Ted Ted Ted Ted Ted

Uma Uma Uma Uma Uma

Urge Urge Urge Urge Urge

Ugo Ugo Ugo Ugo Ugo

Vibe Vibe Vibe Vibe Vibe

Quin

Quiz

Queen

Rise

Ryan

Ruby

Sam

Sean

Seoul

Tune

Talk

Ted

Uma

Urge

Ugo

Vibe

View View View View View

Vicky Vicky Vicky Vicky Vicky

Walk Walk Walk Walk Walk

What What What What What

Will Will Will Will Will

Xbox Xbox Xbox Xbox Xbox

Xeno Xeno Xeno Xeno Xeno

Xena Xena Xena Xena Xena

Yoga Yoga Yoga Yoga Yoga

Yara Yara Yara Yara Yara

Yuna Yuna Yuna Yuna Yuna

Zack Zack Zack Zack Zack

Zoe Zoe Zoe Zoe Zoe

Zone Zone Zone Zone Zone

View

Vicky

Walk

What

Will

Xbox

Xeno

Xena

Yoga

Yara

Yuna

Zack

Zoe

Zone

Write the numbers

1

2

3

4

5

6

7

8

9

10

Notes

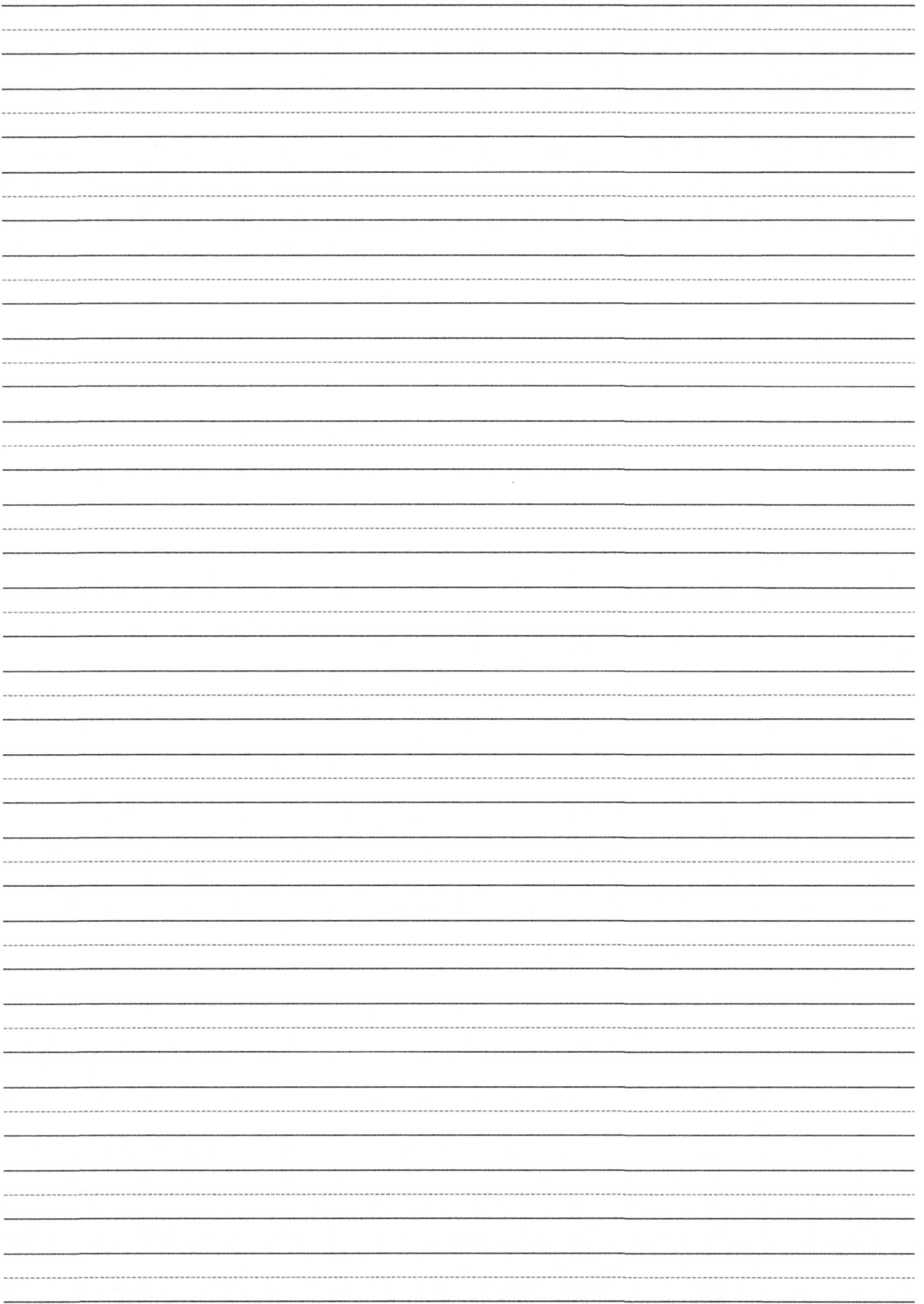

Part 5: Pangrams

Have you ever heard of a pangram? It's a sentence that uses every letter of the alphabet, from A to Z.

You may be familiar with the classic pangram that involves a quick brown fox, but there are many more examples out there. Some of these sentences actually make sense, while others are simply for fun and wordplay.

Our amusing examples in this part are sure to make you laugh and might even inspire you to create your own while improving your cursive handwriting skills.

The five boxing wizards jump quickly.

Pack my box with five dozen liquor jugs.

Two driven jocks help fax my big quiz.

Sphinx of black quartz, judge my vow.

How vexingly quick daft zebras jump.

My ex pub quiz crowd gave joyful thanks.

Bright vixens jump; dozy fowl quack.

The quick brown fox jumps over a lazy dog.

A dozen boxes of rocks were lost in the cyclone.

Sixty zippers were quickly picked from the woven jute bag.

Brown jars prevented the mixture from freezing too quickly.

Watch "Jeopardy!", Alex Trebek's fun TV quiz game.

Farmer Jack realized that big yellow quilts were expensive.

Amazingly few discotheques provide jukeboxes.

The public was amazed to view the quickness and dexterity of the juggler.

The lazy major was fixing Cupid's broken quiver.

Now, your turn to create your own pangrams.

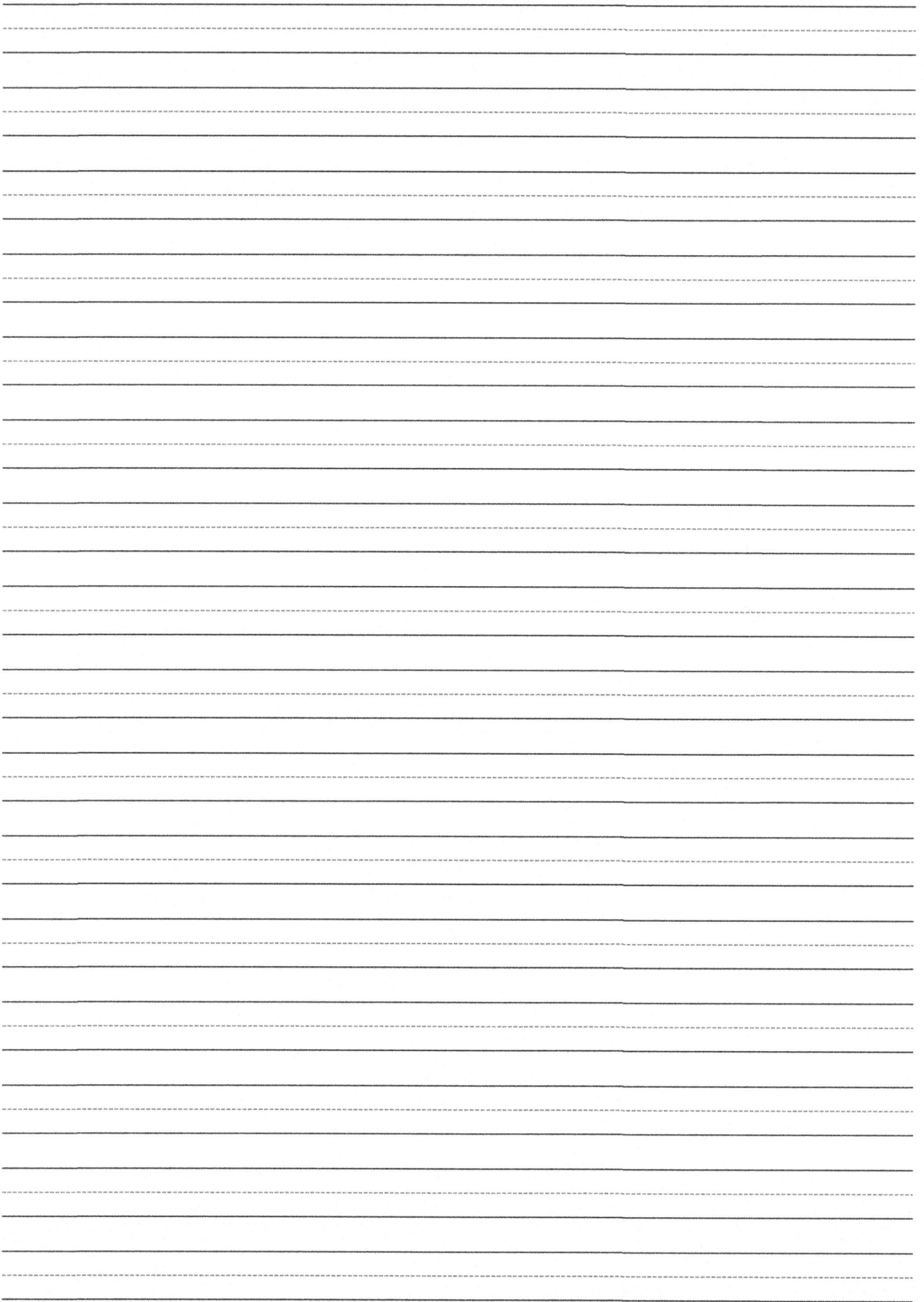

Bonus: Motivational lines

Today is going to be a great day.

Believe in yourself.

No pain, no gain.

Live in the moment.

You are unique.

Create your own sunshine.

Love yourself, flaws and all.

Find joy in the little things.

Everything will be okay in the end.

Keep smiling.

Embrace the journey.

Make memories, not just money.

Be bold or italic. Never be regular.

Never give up on your dreams.

I choose happiness today.

Simplicity is the best.

Stay true to yourself.

Choose love over hate.

Life is a canvas, paint it well.

Trust the magic in you.

Choose kindness, it's always in style.

You can sleep late, eat too much, cry for
no reason and love whoever you want.

Let your day glow with grace.

Say "yes" to what helps you move forward.

Keep your heart open.

You are enough, just as you are.

Find your inner sparkle.

"A flower does not think of competing to the flower next to it. It just blooms."

Sensei Ogui

Here comes free writing. This is your opportunity to let your creativity run wild and showcase the cursive handwriting skills you've been practicing and mastering. Whether you want to write a story, poem, or simply jot down your thoughts and feelings, this is the place to do it.

So take a deep breath, grab your pen and let your imagination take over.

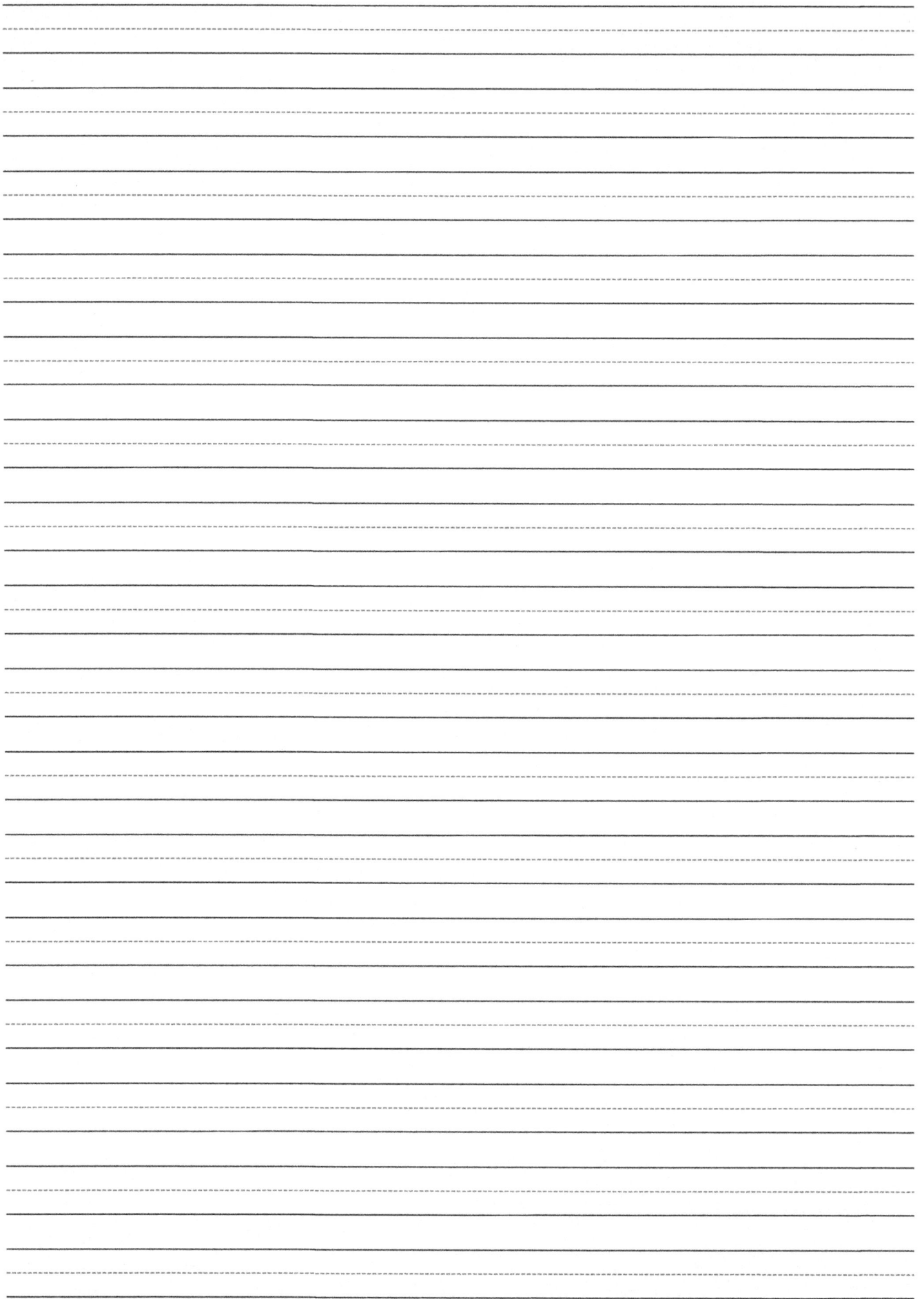

Made in the USA
Las Vegas, NV
28 January 2024